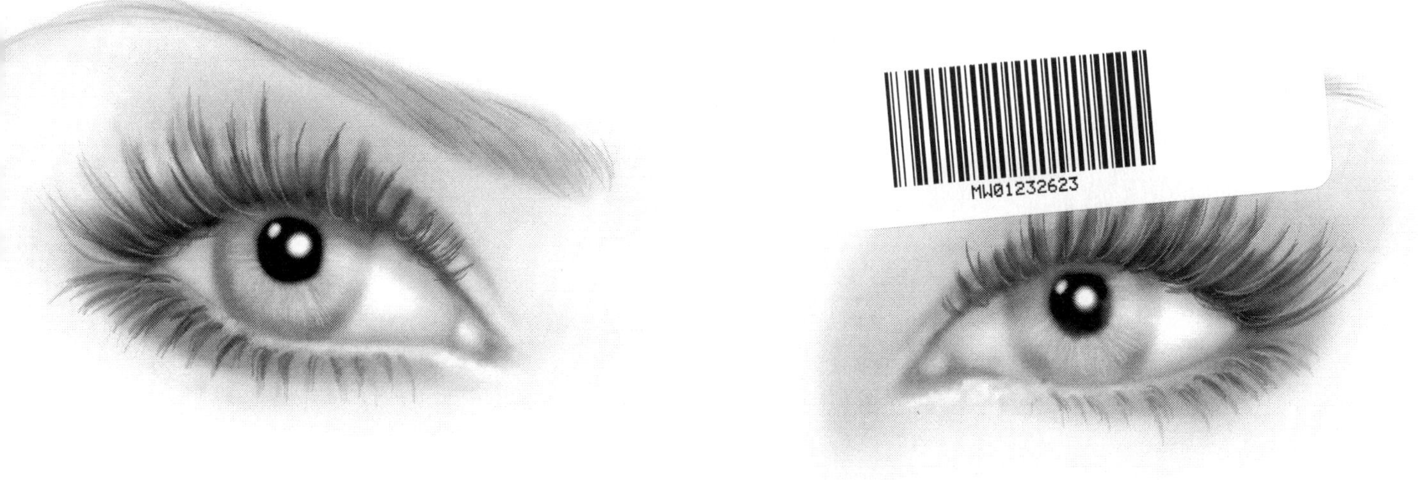

FASHION

COLORING BOOK
Grayscale

includes TWO full sets
of the 23 amazing illustrations

BONUS
9 pictures from
Alena Lazareva's other coloring books

Artworks by
Alena Lazareva

www.alenalazareva.com

Happy coloring!

Share Your Work

Alena Lazareva's Colouring Club

A group for sharing images, inspiration, tips, techniques and more for Alena Lazareva colouring books:
www.facebook.com/groups/alenalazareva/

PARFUM

BONUS

9 of the finest greyscale pictures from my collections of six books:
Amazing coloring book, Fantasy World, Fashion life, Fairies,
Fantasy Kingdom, Sweet Dreams , Winter Wonderland, Mermaids.

Amazing Coloring Book. Grayscale. By Alena Lazareva

Second Set of Pages begins here

Share with a family member, color with a friend
Enjoy coloring your favorite images a second time
Have an extra copy in case you make a mistake

PARFUM

Artist

Alena Lazareva is a artist and illustrator.
Her works had been published in magazines and books of different countries (England, Australia, Italy, Russia). Her main area of focus is fantasy art, mystical beings, fairies and mermaids.

Website: www.alenalazareva.com

Alena Lazareva also has galleries and accounts at:

facebook.com/alenalazareva.art/

instagram.com/artlazareva/

ART PRINTS

High-quality prints, posters, cards, curtains, iPhone cases, pillows, blankets, clocks, bags are available at:
www.zazzle.com/alenalazareva
www.redbubble.com/people/alenalazareva

COLORING BOOKS
by Alena Lazareva

Grayscale Coloring books

Line art Coloring books

amazon

Paperback coloring books:
www.amazon.com/author/alenalazareva

Etsy

PDF(printable coloring pages and books)
www.etsy.com/shop/FantasyAlenaLazareva

Mixed (Grayscale and Line art illustrations)

Made in the USA
San Bernardino, CA
14 July 2020

75435413R00069